Original title:
Roots That Roar

Copyright © 2025 Creative Arts Management OÜ
All rights reserved.

Author: Giselle Montgomery
ISBN HARDBACK: 978-1-80567-347-7
ISBN PAPERBACK: 978-1-80567-646-1

Whirlwinds of the Underground

Down in the soil where the critters play,
Worms have their parties, hip hip hooray!
With a dance in the dark, they wiggle around,
Craving all snacks that get tossed to the ground.

Moles sport their shades, digging tunnels so wide,
While ants in a line form a bumbling ride.
They giggle and grunt, what a raucous affair,
Underneath, life dances without a care.

But watch out for gophers, they're sneaky and sly,
With shovels in hand, they'll wave you goodbye.
While beetles turn cartwheels and let out a cheer,
The underground circus is always quite near.

What fun in the dirt, oh what a grand show,
Where laughter erupts, and the veggies all grow.
So next time you see, just beneath your feet,
Remember the party where all critters meet.

Shadows of the Ancestors

Whispers of figures dancing in gloom,
Old stories arise right out of the tomb.
With hats full of dust, they jiggle and jive,
Past lives that shuffle, oh, how they thrive!

They boast about battles and riches they won,
Still stuck in the past, but they all know how fun.
With ghostly sass, they play tricks from the night,
Making us chuckle with sheer delight.

Behind every shadow, there's laughter in store,
Misfits of history hiding galore.
They poke at our tales with quirky critique,
As we crack up laughing, feeling quite meek.

So raise a glass high to the past's silly crew,
To the shadows who tease and the stories they knew.
For in their wild echoes, we find a bright cheer,
As the memories dance, bringing joy year by year.

A Chorus of the Forgotten

In the attic of time where the dust bunnies feast,\nLurks a
choir of voices, a misfit-like beast.
They croon about scandals and mishaps of yore,
Their harmonies clash, but they always want more.

With misplaced lyrics and a tune gone awry,
Each note is a puzzle, like pie in the sky.
They sing of the blunders that history let slip,
While tripping on phrases, they wiggle and dip.

A cacophony bright, with laughter so loud,
Tunes that could charm even the grumpiest crowd.
In the attic of time, where old meets the new,
A chorus of folly, forever in view.

So join in the revels, let your worries take flight,
Dance with the forgotten until the morn's light.
For in every lost tale, there lives a sweet jest,
As humor and memory blend in a fest.

The Hum of the Unseen

Beneath the floorboards, a ruckus you hear,
Little things buzzing, they're filled with good cheer.
With voices like bees, they conspire and plot,
Creating a symphony of mischief and thought.

In the walls they unite, in shadows they scheme,
They giggle and natter, a comic old dream.
With whispers of wonder and tales that they weave,
The unseen brigade knows how to deceive.

What mischief they make—it's both daft and aloof,
A cadence of chaos, a delightful goof.
So listen with glee to the hum far below,
As laughter and spirit begin to glow.

In every odd creak, a jest waiting there,
Each tinkle of laughter floats softly through air.
With a wink and a nudge, they conjoin their report,
To remind us of fun that we often fall short.

Awakening the Deep

In the soil where secrets play,
They tickle the toes of night and day.
Worms put on a creeping show,
Dancing like they're at a disco.

Mice in capes, oh what a sight,
Throwing parties in the moonlight.
With each burrow, they cheer and play,
As if tomorrow's just a joke to sway.

Ferocity of the Undergrowth

Thorns wear armor, tough and spry,
While cheeky fungi wave goodbye.
The bushes boast of their wild glee,
In a fashion only they can see.

Vines wiggle like they've had too much,
Grabbing passersby with a silly touch.
Each cranny's laughter fills the air,
A jungle gym, without a care.

Song of the Buried Spirits

Down below, they hum a tune,
Chanting softly beneath the moon.
With giggles echoing through the night,
They play peek-a-boo, what a delight!

Bubbles rise from the muddy floor,
As they open a secret door.
A party for those who've gone astray,
Shaking the dust of yesterday.

Untamed Grasp of the Horizon

Look out! The grass waves and shouts,
Telling tales that leave no doubts.
Buzzy bees are the gossip queens,
Spilling secrets of the green machines.

The flowers smile, wear a crown,
While weeds laugh, they won't back down.
Together they form a raucous crew,
With nature's humor, forever anew.

Beneath the Surface

In the ground where secrets lie,
Giggling worms wave them goodbye.
Raccoons hosting tea parties,
While ants dance in tutu farts.

Roots wriggle with glee and grin,
Finding nuts that squirrels skin.
Beetles hoot with laughter,
It's a wild nature's chattering after.

Channels of the Forgotten

In shadows deep, a tale unfolds,
Of squirrels who sing in merry folds.
Trapped in time, forgot the jest,
Until they found a pinecone fest.

Old frogs croak out the news of days,
While moles throw parties in the haze.
Each whisper stirs the ancient ground,
With laughter echoing all around.

The Whirl of Ancestor's Heart

A spin of roots, a twisty dance,
Awakening tales of romance.
A dandelion gives a shout,
As the breezy giggles flout.

Old acorns throw a frisky ball,
While wispy grasses prance through all.
The spirits swirl and hoot with cheer,
In a riotous ancestral theater, dear.

Vibrant Whispers of the Forgotten

Hidden words in whispers sigh,
Where mushrooms wear their hats awry.
Jovial shadows tease the light,
As critters scheme through day and night.

Tales of old in giggles spin,
Mirthful chaos, let the fun begin!
The forest hums in raucous tunes,
Gathering laughter under the moons.

Whispers of the Ground

In a garden where vegetables creep,
They gossip as the breeze makes them leap.
The carrots complain of the beet's long nose,
While the peas tell tales of garden woes.

The radishes tease with their spicy flair,
And the lettuce vows it doesn't have a care.
But when the sun sets, they all break down,
Lamenting their lives, oh, how they frown!

The potatoes roll with laughter and wit,
As they tell the stories of each little hit.
A cucumber chuckles at how it was tossed,
In a salad where its coldness was lost.

Yet beneath the chaos, in silence they scheme,
Planting new mischief, like a dream team.
The garden's alive with a humorous dance,
Where everyone's waiting for their chance!

Echoes Beneath the Surface

Down below, the roots are having all fun,
Chatting and laughing while hiding from sun.
The worms are the judges, with their squiggly flair,
Awarding the prize to the beets with a stare.

The onions are crying, not from sad tales,
But they're tickled pink by their earthy trails.
"Why did the carrot cross over the mound?"
"To show off its orange, all plump and round!"

They whisper of secrets, of growth and of rain,
Chortling at how they all grow through the pain.
"Do you think those sprouts are just pretty and nice?"
"Not when they're covered in mud, oh, that spice!"

So if you ever think soil is bland,
Just peek underground, you'll discover a band.
With laughter so loud it could burst from the earth,
Who knew that such folly had such a great worth?

Vines of Fury

The vines stretch and squabble, entwined in a fight,
Throwing accusations as they shoot for the light.
"Who stole my sunbeam? It's clearly a crime!"
"Get in line, cucumber, your whining's a crime!"

A grape dangles low, all smug with his flair,
While the squash shouts, "You're a berry, beware!"
"You'll get all crushed if you mess with my name,"
Said the chili just simmering, a hot little flame.

The ivy rolls chuckles, twirling up high,
And the peas are just peeking, both shy and spry.
"Let's settle this feud with a race to the hill!"
"On your marks, get set, let's see who's got skill!"

Yet when night falls, they gather around,
With laughter and stories by starlight unbound.
These bickering sprouts in the dark share their dreams,
Transforming their fury into giggling beams.

The Strength of Silent Beginnings

In the dark, where secrets quietly bloom,
A seed whispers softly, breaking its gloom.
"I'd like to stretch and reach for the sky,"
As little roots wiggle, wondering why.

"I'm stuck in this dirt, it's not very grand,"
Complains a lone sprout in a cold, damp land.
"Just wait, oh friend, there's fun up ahead,"
Said the tiny seedling, with dreams in its head.

But when thunder rumbles, they huddle in fright,
As the rain pours down, oh what a sight!
"I was hoping for sunshine, not lakes of despair,"
Grumbled the flowers, while shaking a flare.

Yet all through the storm, they find their own way,
With a giggle or two for the messes they play.
From small, shy beginnings, they rise with great cheer,
For even the quiet have laughter to share!

Embers of the Earth

In the soil, things shake and jive,
Worms do the cha-cha, feeling alive.
Beneath our feet, a party brews,
With dancing sprouts and giggling wasps too.

The daisies wear their party hats,
Mice in tuxedos, just chatting on mats.
Rabbits hop in their Sunday best,
While ants hold a race, and they never rest.

The Deep Breath of Nature

Trees exhale, a burp so loud,
Squirrels giggle, gathering a crowd.
The breeze tickles leaves in a wild dance,
While bees do the tango, taking a chance.

Nature sighs with a comic flair,
Dandelions sneeze, sending seeds in the air.
The sun winks down with a playful glow,
While ladybugs nod in their bright red row.

Unseen Forces

Invisible critters play peek-a-boo,
They whisper secrets the old trees knew.
Raccoons chuckle, plotting their schemes,
While spiders spin nets with glittery dreams.

The grass ticks off toes as you walk,
And mushrooms giggle, starting to talk.
The moon laughs, casting shadows all night,
As the world turns soft, in a comical light.

The Saga Beneath

In the ground, there's a tale so funny,
A gopher in shades counting his money.
Underground parties, where moles take the stage,
With a chorus of crickets from the green page.

A squirrel narrates with a flourish and flair,
As nutshells fly and sparks fill the air.
The roots hum a tune, and the beat drops low,
While the earth chuckles, putting on a show.

Songs of Silent Growth

In the garden, I planted a seed,
Hoping for veggies, but got a weed.
It talks back and demands a raise,
I'm getting outsmarted by my ownWays!

Each morning, I water and fret,
Laughing at vegetables I haven't met.
The radish believes it's a movie star,
While the carrot just waves—quite bizarre!

I thought I was helping, but oh what a twist,
Veggies on strike, they can't be missed.
All I wanted was dinner on a plate,
Now I'm negotiating a veggie date!

I'll bring coffee for the lettuce and peas,
We'll discuss world politics, if you please.
Who knew that growing them could be a chore?
Next time, I'll just buy from the store.

The Power Within

Deep underground, where the secrets lie,
A potato is dreaming of flying high.
It's growing wings—yes, in its mind,
Hoping to leave the dirt far behind!

Carrots play twister, digging for fun,
While onions are crying, but it's all in good pun.
Each stem has a story, complex and neat,
In the soil, they gossip and dance on their feet!

The garlic is plotting an escape,
While broccoli plans to make some cape.
In this lively world, they banter and jest,
Who knew growing food could be like a fest?

So next time you chew on that salad so crisp,
Remember, it's a meeting, a very wild trip.
The power within, it's depth and it's cheer,
Is grounded in laughter, a truth that's so clear!

Ties to the Past

In the attic, a root vegetable found,
A decade-old memory, still stuck in the ground.
It's whispering tales of the meals that were made,
Of chilly nights or a grand garden parade!

A tomato with stories of summers long gone,
Exclaims, "Hey, I was the star! Remember it's dawn?"
With flavor so rich, it stood proud and tall,
Until it turned sauce with a clamoring call!

The peas, once green, now sing of romance,
Of love in the kitchen, a stir and a dance.
Broccoli reminisces of dinosaurs brave,
In the name of salad, it decided to pave!

So when we munch on our lunches divine,
Remember those whispers from plants in their prime.
Each bite has a history, a giggle, a laugh,
As we feast on the past, served humble on half!

Veins of Verdant Wisdom

There's a sage in the soil with roots that confide,
In a world with no wifi, it's wisdom worldwide.
The cucumbers argue, but I can't complain,
With veggies so wise, there's no need for disdain!

The lettuce, a scholar, with leaves so profound,
Studies the weather, with weather profound.
"Cloudy today? A leafy parade!"
Let's groove to the rhythm Mother Nature's made!

The peppers dish gossip, each colorful tale,
While eggplant's just waiting for someone to hail.
With laughter and humor, they spread their great charm,
As I dig my hands deep, they warm up my arm!

So when you see veggies, just know what they say,
They're plotting and planning, in their leafy ballet.
With wisdom like a forest, and humor they share,
Life in the garden is fabulously rare!

Reverberations of the Earth

Beneath the soil, a ticklish dance,
Worms in tuxedos take a chance.
Squirrels gossip under moonlit skies,
While moles throw shade in clever guise.

Rivers giggle, rocks tumble down,
Trees wear crowns, oh what a gown!
Clouds puff up with giggly glee,
As ants parade in a jolly spree.

Boulders sing in booming tones,
While hedgehogs drop their royal phones.
Fungi share their secret tales,
Of mushroom parties with silly gales.

The underground's a silly place,
Where laughter echoes in every space.
With each thud of thunder, a chuckle's born,
Nature winks, and the world is torn.

Fierce Tendrils of Time

In gardens, vines twist with a cheer,
They wrestle as tomatoes leer.
Cabbages cloak themselves in style,
As turnips dance a jaunty mile.

Time travels down the leafy lane,
Saplings giggle at the rain.
The herbs exchange the silliest puns,
While flowerbeds make popcorn runs.

Thorns try to be the garden's king,
But daffodils start to sing.
The stakes are high, the stakes are fun,
When clover crowns everyone!

Each petal rhymes a tale untold,
As sprouts plan bold jokes and jesters bold.
With every hour, they tick and tock,
In this garden, laughter's the greatest stock.

Heartbeats Underground

Deep in the dirt, the rhythm's strong,
Earthworms wiggle to a funky song.
Gophers tap dance, it's quite a sight,
While ghosts of plants join in the night.

Mice in boots do a jitterbug,
And daisies give each other a hug.
The soil's pulse is lively and bright,
As roots chuckle at the moon's white light.

Beetles bring a raucous sound,
With every thump, the laughter's found.
The pulse of life is full of cheer,
As all the critters gather near.

Beneath our feet, it's wild and free,
Where laughs and beats create harmony.
Dig down deep, don't be shy,
Join the party where dirt meets the sky!

The Legacy of Unseen Forces

In darkened corners, shadows dance,
Whispers flutter, a lively prance.
The spirits of plants weave in and out,
Painting stories with joyful shout.

Starlight twinkles with ghostly glee,
As roots and skits play hide and seek.
Every breeze shares a funny tale,
Of nature's antics and winds that wail.

The ground holds secrets, oh so grand,
With giggling gnomes that make a stand.
The legacy left is laughter's song,
Where everything silly feels so strong.

So join in the mirth, take a bow,
The unseen forces are here, somehow!
Beneath our feet, the fun swells wide,
In this wild world where silliness bides.

Ancestral Echoes in the Mist

In the fog, my grandpa's face,
Tells me tales of a silly race.
He chased a squirrel, slipped on a log,
Then blamed it all on a friendly dog.

Great-Aunt Betty danced on a chair,
While Uncle Fred lost his best underwear.
Confetti flew from a pie in the sky,
All our secrets in laughter fly.

I swear one time, great grandpa sneezed,
And everyone there just felt so pleased.
They laughed and snorted, spilled their drinks,
What wisdom lays, sometimes it stinks!

Echoes linger with chuckles and cheer,
Each memory wraps me, warm yet clear.
Though mist may hide their silly pranks,
In my heart, I give them all my thanks.

Warlike Vines of Fortune

In the garden, they boldly clash,
The weeds and flowers all make a splash.
Petunias arm with spiked defense,
While dandelions plot their recompense.

My tomato plants wear knightly gear,
Defending against pests, full of cheer.
Rabbits try sneaking, quick as a flash,
But lettuce leads them to a trashy bash.

Cucumbers joust with overripe pride,
While eggplants serve as the court's good side.
Bell peppers throw shade, a colorful bar,
In this veggie war, no one's a star.

Yet as they battle with quite the flair,
I can't help but just stop and stare.
In this fierce garden, I find delight,
In all their struggles, a humorous sight.

Echoes Beneath the Surface

Beneath the soil, a choir sings,
Of worms debating the latest things.
They bicker on the tastiest dirt,
While ants parade in their little shirt.

A beetle boasts of a treasure find,
While grubs giggle, so unconfined.
'What's the best way to tunnel deep?'
'Avoid the cat, or lose your leap!'

In the dark with roots entwined,
They swap old stories, one of a kind.
Like tiny jesters, they push and shove,
The underground—oh what a love!

Yet when the rain begins to fall,
They rally together, one and all.
With muddy antics and joyful cheer,
Life's a comedy when nature's near.

Whispers of the Underground

In the shadows, a gossip spread,
'Did you hear what the onion said?'
Cauliflower blushing, they turn away,
While radishes giggle and dance in play.

The carrots debate their length and style,
'Look at my orange, isn't it vile?'
But beets chime in with a cheeky grin,
'At least I'm not a turnip, my kin!'

Secret meetings held underneath,
Where mushrooms plot with a cunning sheath.
They scheme and dream of the rain above,
In this dark world, there's nothing but love.

Yet when the gardener takes her stride,
The whispers hush, all must decide.
With quick escapes in the soft, wet mud,
Life in the ground—oh, a happy thud!

Grounded Echoes

In the garden, gnomes do dance,
Wiggling wildly, taking a chance.
They shake their shovels, oh so spry,
Yelling nonsense as they fly by.

Earthworms party in their own way,
Grooving underground, night and day.
When daisies laugh, it's quite a sight,
Drinking the dew, they sip with delight.

A beetle dressed in a tiny hat,
Claims he's the king, imagine that!
With every buzz and every wink,
They live their lives before we think.

So here's to dirt and all its cheer,
Where mischief grows, never near fear.
With every laugh that springs from earth,
A giggle's worth more than its girth.

Ancient Calls from the Dark

A tree once said, 'I'm wise, you see,'
While squirrels argued with glee,
They chattered loudly, holding their ground,
The wittiest banter ever found.

From roots below, a whisper cracked,
Old branches swayed, and leaves unpacked.
They jest about the bugs that bite,
Telling tales 'til the moon's goodnight.

A shadowy owl hooted for fun,
'Why stay awake when the day's already done?'
His buddies laughed, owls in a stitch,
"Let's hoot at the stars and make a glitch!"

So beneath the covers of night so bright,
Giggles echo, sparkling the fright.
With laughter drawn from centuries past,
Old trees remind us to have a blast.

The Whispered Wind

The wind told secrets to the leaves,
A tale of giggles sprouting from eves.
It tickled flowers and ruffled fur,
'The sun's a comedian, that's for sure!'

As grasses danced with unsteady glee,
They whispered back, 'Hey, look at me!'
Each breeze a jester, swaying stout,
Unraveling joy 'til the dusk comes out.

And when the clouds began to pout,
The raindrops joined in with a shout.
'Hey, silly sun, don't be so shy,
Let's make laughter light up the sky!'

So here we find, in nature's play,
Joy resides in each gentle sway.
In every gust and flurry of fun,
The Earth keeps spinning, 'til day is done.

The Depths Resound

Beneath the soil, a chatter blooms,
With worms debating in leafy rooms.
"I saw a boot!" one critter claims,
"I found a shoe to play our games!"

Rocky walls hum a silly tune,
While stalactites tap-dance 'neath the moon.
They giggle as shadows squish and squirm,
And ghostly echoes twist and worm.

Rabbits burrow deep with flair,
Telling tales of snacks they'll share.
"I heard the carrots have a party,
Let's hop on over, don't be tardy!"

So deep below, where laughter glows,
The Earth's a stage where humor flows.
With every wiggle and little sound,
In the depths of fun, joy is found.

Tides Beneath the Surface

In the depths where fish do play,
A clam once dreamed of running away.
It donned a shell that sparkled bright,
A glittering suit brought quite a fright.

It waddled out with quite a flair,
To dance like seaweed in the air.
But with each twirl and every spin,
A hungry turtle grinned with a grin.

The clam declared, "I've got my game!"
But felt so silly, wasn't that lame?
With laughter echoing through the blue,
It slid back home, and cheered "Woohoo!"

Now in the depths, our clam will stay,
And ponder lightly, in its own way.
That fanciful dreams can tug you about,
But home is the best, without a doubt.

The Silent Legacy

In the garden, whispers bloom,
Where daisies plot and tangle loom.
A sunflower wore a mighty crown,
And made the other flowers frown.

"Why are you so tall?" they croaked,
"With necks so long, we're all provoked!"
But sunflower just giggled low,
"I reach for sunshine, you know?"

Morning glories crept with stealth,
They whispered plans to steal its wealth.
"A tall tale's brewing—watch me rise!"
They popped up quickly, oh, what a surprise!

Yet with each twist and every turn,
The sunflower laughed, for it would learn.
That blooms can compete, or just be merry,
In gardens vast and kitchen very.

Bound by the Earth

A wise old tree had quite the view,
Its branches waved to me and you.
It watched the squirrels chase their tails,
While telling tales of ancient trails.

"Once I was young and spry," it said,
"I danced with breezes, then sowed my bed.
But now I'm stuck right here, you see,
With birds as my guests, how fancy free!"

The ground shook once with thunder's clap,
That little tree took quite a nap.
When it awoke, the world was bent,
But in its heart, it just laughed and went.

So dance, oh branches, sway with flair,
For roots run deep, yet dreams can air.
Even when bound to earthy shallows,
Find joy in life, like chirping swallows.

The Call of the Hidden

Beneath the soil where secrets dwell,
The gophers giggle, 'Oh, what the hell!'
They dig and dash with shovels bold,
For treasures of gold—well, at least, some mold.

Once they found a funky sock,
That smelled like cheese and made them mock.
With giggles loud, they planned a quest,
To find more laughs and do their best.

"Let's catch a worm to launch our spree!"
The bravest shouted, "Wait for me!"
But squirmy worms are wise and slick,
They vanished quick, just like a trick!

At dusk they munched on roots and greens,
While sharing tales of wacky scenes.
"Who knew being buried could be such fun?
Let's dig some more—our day's just begun!"

Echos from Below

In the ground they wiggle and sway,
Beneath our feet, they dance all day.
They whisper tales, but who can hear?
A pickle jar, or maybe a beer?

When plants are bored, they'll tell a joke,
About a tree that couldn't smoke.
The laughter bubbles, quite the sound,
As laughter rises from underground.

In soil's embrace, they throw a feast,
With worms and bugs, to say the least.
They gossip loudly, make no fuss,
While we just stare, oh, what's the rush?

When night falls down, they hold a ball,
With fungi twirls, they have a ball.
A root parade, in leafy caps,
All cavorting in nature's laps.

The Thrum of the Timberlands

Deep in the woods, they'll jam and play,
With sap and bark, they steal the day.
They groove like crazy, trunks all sway,
The squirrels join in, and it's a ballet!

When the vines try to show off moves,
They trip on twigs, oh, how they bruise!
The leafy crowds will cheer them on,
With laughter echoing until dawn.

Branches waving, the birds take flight,
As trees make jokes, oh what a sight!
"Why don't we ever get out for lunch?"
"Because we're rooted, and it packs a punch!"

So come on down, join the ruckus,
They'll serve you tea in a fine old circus.
With every thrum, life's a delight,
In the timberlands, day turns to night.

Layers of Living History

Beneath the surface lies a tale,
Of ancient times and ships that sail.
The boots of giants, once so grand,
Now buried deep within the sand.

With every layer, stories grow,
Of long-lost socks and fancy bows.
A history book, but underground,
Just waiting for us to dig around.

A fossilized chef, he cooked for ants,
With recipes that caused quite the dance.
Each shovel full, a giggle's worth,
From pudding stones to chocolate mirth.

So bring a spoon and dig on down,
To find lost treasures without a frown.
For buried laughter is the best,
In layers deep, we find the jest.

The Voice of the Subterranean

Down below, they have a band,
With mushrooms strumming, oh so grand.
The notes rise up like bubbles bright,
A concert hidden from our sight.

"Excuse me, sir, do you want to dance?"
Said the radish in his spiffy pants.
With beetroot beats and cauliflower cheer,
They invite you down, come join the sphere!

The fungus man, he tells some jokes,
About the life of carrots and yolks.
The soil giggles, full of mirth,
As veggies roll with happy girth.

So if you pause and lend an ear,
You'll hear them laughter, loud and clear!
For in the ground, where all is slight,
There's fun galore in the earth's delight.

Awakening the Forgotten

In a garden of gnomes, quite spry,
Lurks a potato, oh my, oh my.
He dreams of a dance with the sun,
But gets tangled up, oh what fun!

Twirling weeds sing songs of their kin,
While ants form a line, where to begin?
A carrot's got jokes, but they're mostly corny,
And the radishes blush in all their glory.

Toadstools giggle at thunder's loud clap,
While daisies pretend they're in a great rap.
The grass tickles toes beneath the sky,
As all join the dance, oh please don't be shy!

A thistle in tutus leads the parade,
With chants of joy, the garden's well-played.
A rabbit with shades shows off his new moves,
In this wild gathering, everyone grooves!

Ferocious Whispers from Below

Deep in the soil, a treasure lies,
Worms share gossip, oh what a surprise!
They twist and they turn with great flair,
While grubs tell tales, hoping for air.

Moles drafting plans to break through the scene,
Proposing a party—oh, they're quite keen.
The beetles debate who's the best dancer,
While snails play poker with questionable answers.

A frisky young root shouts, 'Let's dig!'
His friends cheer him on, each feeling quite big.
Mud pies are flung at the sun up above,
With laughter and chaos, it's what they all love!

Squirrels above get a front-row seat,
As the underground party can't be beat.
With giggles and grumbles, they join in the play,
As whispers from below make the world sway!

The Hidden Symphony of Strength

Beneath the surface, a concert unfolds,
With veggies as musicians, brave and bold.
Carrots on violins strum with delight,
While onions provide the bass, holding tight.

Cabbages sway in harmonious glee,
As radishes tap with their roots, oh so free.
Potatoes stomp to the beat of the drum,
The rhythm of soil, oh how it does thrum!

Chorus of seedlings join in the cheer,
Singing of growth, for spring is so near.
A dandelion makes a sweet solo call,
As bees buzz in tune, oh they've come for a ball!

Yet through it all, the weeds raise their hand,
Lamenting their fate with a sad, silly band.
But in this grand night, they blend with the throng,
In this hidden symphony, everyone belongs!

Beyond the Bark: A Roar

The trees take their turn, striking a pose,
With squirrels on stage, everyone knows.
A trunk does a twist, branches go wild,
While the oak sings a tune like a curious child.

"Watch my bark!" one tree shouts with flair,
As little birds giggle, "You just need some hair!"
A pine needles nod in rhythmic delight,
Chiming in, "Let's party under the moonlight!"

A breezy whisper jokes of old logs,
As branches are dancing with all of the frogs.
The mushrooms giggle at the great tire swing,
Celebrating the joy that a forest can bring!

With laughter and shadows, the night awoke,
As nature's own circus, beneath the oak.
A gathering lower than the sky above,
In this woodland party, there's nothing but love!

The Awakening Soil

Beneath the ground, a party raves,
Worms do the cha-cha, the soil behaves.
Ants in tuxedos, they dance on the mound,
Every leaf and rock joins the sound.

Once a stale plot, now a whimsical scene,
Where moles wear hats and the toads are keen.
Critters gossip, gossip, you wouldn't believe,
Even the daisies shake their leaves.

Sunshine spills laughter, rain drops a beat,
Caterpillars groove on their little green feet.
The earth is alive, it's a jolly affair,
With nature's own humor bubbling in air.

So next time you tread on the soft, squishy bed,
Remember the jokes that the soil has said.
For life underground is a jest to explore,
Where each tiny whisper is anything but a bore.

Unseen Echoes of Strength

In the shadows, roots chuckle and shout,
While trees above wear hats made of clout.
Branches bow low, as if they could hear,
The whispers of friends, making laughter near.

Mighty oaks share tales of the leaves,
Who dared to surf on the summer's eaves.
Their jokes travel down, through the twine,
A secret society, simply divine.

With every breeze, they boast and they tease,
Waving to each other with rhythmic ease.
Fungi join hands, a merry old crew,
Celebrating strength in their underground stew.

So when you stand tall, beneath their vast shade,
Don't forget the humor that's quietly laid.
The unseen connections, so clever and spry,
Would tickle your fancy if only they'd try.

The Fiber of Connection

With strands of laughter woven so tight,
The twine of the earth dances with delight.
Spiders spin jokes in their silken finesse,
While grasses gossip in their green velvet dress.

The bumblebees buzz in a playful parade,
As frogs bring the tunes, a raucous serenade.
Through tangled tendrils of camaraderie,
A friendship so strong, yet light as a leaf.

Cacti take selfies in the morning glow,
While daisies debate who's the fairest, you know.
Their roots intertwined, a comical stew,
They jest about how they both sprout and grew.

So join their confab, immerse in the play,
In the bouncy basement where friendships sway.
For every fiber that connects and may hold,
Is a tale worth telling, a jest to be told.

Resounding in the Depths

In the earth's cozy café, whispers abound,
With gophers as baristas, the best drinks around.
They serve up some humor with each little sip,
Roots telling jokes, with a riotous quip.

Tapping into the humor where no one can see,
Wisdom cascades like a whimsical spree.
The laughter erupts from the soil's deep core,
As laughter and strength blend to roar.

With spores making puns, how delightful it seems,
While vines weave tales from their dreamiest dreams.
In this secretive space where no eyes can pry,
A carnival of jest just dances on by.

So when you look up, at the trees so grand,
Remember the giggles that spring from the sand.
For beneath the surface, there's joy overflowing,
A world of laughter, endlessly glowing.

The Power Beneath Our Feet

Beneath the ground, they wiggle and jiggle,
A party of soil, with space to giggle.
Tap-dancing fungi in bowlers and sprigs,
They toast to the worms, and the joys of the digs.

Outrageous greens with a funky design,
The carrots tell jokes while sipping on brine.
Potatoes sport hats, just bursting with flair,
Each veggie a joker, without a care!

The daisies compete for the loudest of laughs,
While radishes blush, cutting up with the gaffs.
In this underground circus, the fun has a beat,
The power's alive, right beneath your feet!

So next time you stroll on that grass so spry,
Remember the party that's happening nigh.
With wiggles and jiggles, they truly do play,
Beneath us, the laughter is here every day.

Ancestral Stories in the Dark

In the midnight soil, where shadows convene,
A caper of critters, a wacky routine.
Grandpa's old stories, now tangled with cheers,
As gophers chuckle, swapping ancient smears.

The moles tap their toes, beneath the night's crest,
With wit that eludes the worst of their jest!
Bats flit around, with a wink and a nod,
As tales of old Harold, make even trees applaud!

Under the moonlight, in whispers so clear,
The baggage of centuries brings laughter near.
They riddle and giggle, oh, what a delight,
In this sunken soirée, it's a raucous night!

So take a moment, and lend them your ear,
Their stories of humor, you'll find quite sincere.
With chuckles and wisdom from dark-hued pasts,
These ancestral tales are too fun to outlast!

Thunderous Roots of the Past

In the wild, wild woods, where the whispers ignite,
The past raises eyebrows, oh what a sight!
Trees strutting their stuff, with an old-fashioned glee,
Wearing beards made of moss, just as spry as can be.

From acorns to oaks, each one has a tale,
Of squirrels in capes and a porcupine frail.
They dance with the breeze, make a racket and roar,
Reminding the chipmunks, there's always room for more!

Their laughter is rumbling, a thunderous cheer,
The maple's got jokes that'll make you shed a tear.
Each ring holds a secret of giggles and glee,
While blossoms are blushing, oh, you can't help but see!

So, next time you trek through the ancient expanse,
Join in on the fun, and give nature a chance.
With trees and their tales, you'll find quite a blast,
In the thunderous echoes of ages long passed!

The Silent Roar of Nature

In tranquil green fields, a silence that gleams,
But watch in amazement, at what nature dreams.
The daisies are plotting, with laughter so sly,
As the grasses all gossip, while tufts wave goodbye.

A mighty oak whispers to the cheeky breeze,
"Those critters best watch, I'll bend them with ease!"
With a chuckle, the willows throw shade on the ants,
While squirrels get rowdy in glittery pants!

The petals all giggle, with smiles so bright,
As shadows do tango in the cool of the night.
Silently roaring, in a whimsical way,
Nature's a comedian, come join in the play!

So tiptoe and listen, there's fun to be shown,
In the silent-filled laughter of the trees that have grown.
With whispers and giggles, they call out a cheer,
Nature's alive, and its humor is clear!

Journey of Inner Echoes

In the depths where giggles grow,
A ticklish tick-tock starts the show.
Whispers of laughter twist and turn,
Echoes of joy in a curious spurn.

Belly buttons dance with cheer,
Finding humor far and near.
Puns sprout up from hidden nooks,
Like silly stunts from old comic books.

Socks that don't match join the spree,
A whimsy parade of glee!
Each chuckle a note in delight,
As inner echoes take off in flight.

So come along, and take a peek,
A merry place where giggles speak.
With every twist, new fun unfolds,
A journey of laughter, worth more than gold.

The Dynamic Depth

Beneath the surface, mischief brews,
Cartwheeling thoughts, in colorful hues.
A plunge into giggles, a splash of cheer,
Dynamic depths that draw us near.

Bubbles of humor rising fast,
Floating around, they won't be last.
Flip-flops chatter in underwater jokes,
Even the fish are laughing folks!

Twists and turns, a whirlpool of fun,
Where serious thoughts dare not run.
Ticklish tides and a droll plight,
In the dynamic depths, we dance in delight.

So take the plunge, let laughter swell,
In this watery world, we know so well.
With every splash, a story to tell,
Dynamic depth, where joy rings a bell.

Cadence of the Hidden

In shadows where silliness creeps,
A beat of chuckles, and silence peeps.
Secrets wrapped in giggly tunes,
Dancing beneath the watchful moon.

Whispers of humor in hushed delight,
Sneaking around like a cheeky sprite.
A subtle jiggle hides in the air,
Cadence of laughter everywhere!

Stifled snickers and snorts that sprout,
In each hidden nook, they twist about.
With every giggle, the silence breaks,
A symphony born from joyful mistakes.

So listen closely to the sneak,
The cadence of joy speaks loud and meek.
In the hidden corners, laughter thrives,
A rhythmic tune that tickles our lives.

Rooted in Silence

In quiet corners where silence plays,
A riot of thoughts in mischievous ways.
Whispers of wit in hushed embrace,
Life's subtle jokes that make us race.

Tangled secrets in muffled glee,
Each laugh like a bee buzzing free.
A ticklish thought beneath the fold,
Hidden treasures, worth more than gold.

Muffled chortles in a shushing room,
Escape the gloom, let laughter bloom.
Chasing whispers that tickle our ears,
In the hush of joy, we dance without fears.

So venture deep into the calm,
Find the humor, sweet like a balm.
In silence, the silliest pranks take flight,
Rooted in quiet, oh what a night!

Strength in Shadows

In dark corners, secrets laugh,
A potato dressed up as a gaffe.
Whispers of courage, silly yet bright,
Spooked the shadows all through the night.

A squirrel with dreams of being a king,
Dances around with a gleeful swing.
With nutty determination, he strives,
In the shadows, true strength survives.

When sunlight fades and giggles creep,
The silly thoughts dive in deep.
Hilarity blooms where fear was formed,
In the shadows, fun is warmed.

So raise a cheer for the goofy light,
That dances along with all its might.
For in the dark, where laughter grows,
Strength in shadows, oh, how it glows!

The Legacy of the Lifeblood

Grandma's stew, a bubbling fall,
Brings everyone together for the call.
With funny bones and laughter loud,
Each drop of broth makes us proud.

From the garden, veggies vie for fame,
Tomatoes arguing, 'Who's to blame?'
In the pot, a spicy debate,
A recipe of joy we celebrate.

A loaf of bread sings to the tune,
Of dancing crumbs, a floury boon.
With every slice, a giggle is shared,
In the legacy, love is declared.

So when we feast on life's sweet bread,
Each funny story fills our heads.
The bond we share, forever woven tight,
In the laughter's glow, everything feels right!

The Silent Symphony

In gardens lush, where veggies hum,
A carrot sings with a cheeky strum.
Beets play drums, with bubbles and pops,
As the corn on the cob does hip-hop flops.

Frogs in the pond, croaking their tune,
Join the rhythm beneath the moon.
With every splash, hilarity swells,
Nature's concert, where laughter dwells.

Crickets chirp in a jazzy way,
While daisies sway and dance the day.
Each note a giggle, each leaf a cheer,
In silence, music is crystal clear.

So let us join this silly song,
Where funny grows, we all belong.
In the symphony of giggles we find,
The heart of laughter, wonderfully blind!

Beneath the Giants

Under the trees, with trunks so wide,
Squirrels hold court, let laughter preside.
Acorns drop, like comedic stones,
As the forest giggles at its own bones.

A wise old owl, with glasses so thick,
Tells jokes to the rabbits, loud and quick.
"Why did the leaf fall? For a root beer spree!"
Giggles erupt, oh, how fun to be.

The shadows twist, with mischief in store,
As raccoons plot to start a dance floor.
Tiny creatures create quite the scene,
Shaking their tails, the forest is keen.

So dwell beneath giants, where whimsy grows,
In the heart of nature, the laughter flows.
For among the trees, with humor so bright,
Life's a funny tale, a pure delight!

Vines of Vicissitude

In the garden, plants debate,
Who will grow tall, who will be late?
The daisies giggle, the roses jive,
While cucumbers dance, so alive!

A salad forms a band on the lawn,
With lettuce strumming till the dawn.
Tomatoes join in, feeling quite spry,
While radishes just wave goodbye!

As the wind whispers a comical tale,
Of how sunflowers never fail.
With their heads held high, they cause a stir,
While worms below just laugh and purr!

So next time you see a flower in bloom,
Remember the jokes in the garden's room.
In each tiny sprout and leafy display,
Are the giggles of nature, come out to play!

The Echoes of Endurance

The old oak tree sways with glee,
As squirrels scamper with no degree.
'I'm sturdy!' it boasts, 'Though winds may blow,
I've weathered storms—just look at my fro!'

Crickets chirp a hilarious tune,
While shadows dance under the moon.
'You think you're tough?' a beetle will shout,
As it tumbles around, giving a rout!

With roots so deep, they whisper 'Hey!
Life's a joke, come join the fray!'
As flowers tape their petals tight,
For a comedy show that lasts all night!

So laugh with the leaves, let humor unfold,
Nature's tales are treasures, pure gold.
In every sway and every shift,
Are echoes of laughter, a gravity lift!

Shadows of the Sylvan

In the forest, shadows mingle with cheer,
A deer trips lightly, with nothing to fear.
'Watch me!' it calls, taking a leap,
While legs go flailing—a tumble so deep!

Branches chatter with a tick-tock sound,
As morning light spills all around.
'Did you hear that?' a wise old owl,
Says, 'Did the fox just try to howl?'

Frogs orchestrate the funniest croak,
While trees shake their leaves, 'Was that a joke?'
Mushrooms giggle, tucked in their beds,
As sunlight tickles their tiny heads!

So, join the dance where shadows play,
Every bark and squeak leads to a sway.
Amidst the fun and dappled light,
The sylvan spirits keep laughing bright!

Heartbeats Underfoot

Beneath our feet, the critters scheme,
With fuzzy dreams and a vibrant theme.
A mole throws a party, 'Come one, come all!'
As ants form a conga line, oh what a ball!

The worm does the twist, oh what a sight,
As grasshoppers hop with sheer delight.
'This soil is our stage!' the beetles exclaim,
While earthworms play an underground game!

Each heartbeat pulses in rhythm and rhyme,
With nature's orchestra, spinning through time.
So when you walk, just tap your feet,
And join the party, life's a treat!

In every step, a dance unfolds,
With laughter shared and stories retold.
For underfoot, the magic's alive,
With heartbeat antics that help us thrive!

Offshoots of Resilience

In the garden, a sprout grew tall,
With a wig made of leaves, it had a ball.
It danced in the breeze, oh what a sight,
Chasing worms at dawn, oh what a delight!

From cracks in the pavement, life finds a way,
Making friends with a weed in a playful display.
They giggle and wiggle, under sun's bright gaze,
Turning asphalt jungles into funny maze!

With each little bit of sun and of rain,
They shout, "We're the champions, free from the chain!"
Their laughter bursts forth from branches so spry,
"You can't clip our wings, we're too tough to die!"

So next time you wander, keep a keen eye,
For the rascals beneath, who reach for the sky.
In funny little ways, they'll make you chuckle,
Life's a banquet of laughs, wrapped in green snuggle!

The Voice of the Undergrowth

In shadows they shimmer, the lowly ferns,
With shy little giggles, for sunlight they yearn.
They murmur and chatter, their secrets so sly,
"Who needs a tall tale when you're close to the sky?"

The mushrooms all moan, in a humorous way,
"I sprouted last night, what a surprise day!"
And the crickets add in, with a chorus so loud,
"Who needs a stage when you're part of a crowd?"

The foxgloves flip-flop in a whimsical style,
Dressed up in colors, they dance for a while.
"Oh, look at us sway!" they proclaim with a cheer,
We're the voices of soil, come join us right here!"

So listen quite closely, as the undergrowth sings,
A concert of laughter, on unlikely wings.
Life's a funny venture through thick and through thin,
Where humor and growth become one big grin!

Life Beneath

Down in the dark, where the funny folks play,
Worms throw a party at the end of the day.
With roots as their confetti, they wiggle and jig,
"Who needs a disco? Let's dance in the big!"

The beetles are beetling, with hats made of leaves,
Sipping on dew, while the grass softly weaves.
"Pass me a snack—those old seeds look so neat!"
A feast of the underground, oh what a treat!

The moles bring the music with thumping delight,
Thumping and jumping, they dance out of sight.
"No need for a reason; we're masters of fun,"
"Let's celebrate life till the morning has come!"

So next time you ponder what's beneath garden sod,
Just remember the laughter from beings un-awed.
Life thrives in the darkness, with quips and with roars,
Where joy and good humor forever endures!

Symphony of the Soil

Each seed is a player, each root is a chord,
Together they weave an orchestra adored.
"Can you hear us?" they sing, "We're the band underground!
With bass in the compost and treble all around!"

The daisies hum softly while the grasses sway,
Making melodies in a most quirky way.
The ants clap their hands, keeping time on the beat,
While the earthworms enjoy a symphonic treat!

"Hey there, dear squirrel! Come join in the fun,
We'll serenade you under the bright summer sun!"
With a tickle of roots and a whisper of leaves,
They make music together—oh what a reprieve!

In this symphony grand, all critters partake,
From the tiniest sprout to the old giant oak.
So next time you wander, stop just for a glance,
And join in the laughter, come join in the dance!

Threads of Tenacity

In the tangled mess of hidden strands,
A squirrel leaps, with acorns in hands.
It tugs on fibers, oh what a scene,
Waging war with dust bunnies, what a routine!

The daisies laugh, they're watching the show,
As earthworms wiggle, putting on a toe.
Their dance is messy, but all in good cheer,
Who knew chaos could have such a sneer?

Up from the mulch, a thistle takes flight,
Singing weird tunes in the middle of night.
A chorus of critters joins in the song,
With a beat so catchy, you can't help but throng!

So here's to the threads that twist and they twine,
Creating such fun in this world so divine.
With laughter and giggles, they anchor and sway,
A riot of joy, come dance and play!

The Oath of the Deep

In the shadows below, the fish all conspire,
To hold a grand banquet, adorned with their fire.
Jellyfish glow like candles of glee,
While crabs perform ballet in front of a tree!

A clam stands up and clears out its throat,
Says 'Please don't eat me, I'm not just a coat!'
The octopus chuckles, he's crafty and sly,
While sea cucumbers just sit by and cry.

The eels start to groove, doing the twist,
With anemones dancing, you get the gist.
A fishy debate, who gets the last fry?
The shrimp take a vote while puffers just sigh.

So raise up your fins and make a grand cheer,
For the sea life that gathers each brightening year.
In the depths of the ocean, where laughter won't stop,
They're weaving connections, never to drop!

Embraces from the Earth

A bear in pajamas sings soft to the ground,
As daisies join in with their sweet little sound.
They tickle the toes of the trees up above,
Spreading the gossip, oh what a love!

The roots below whisper secrets so dear,
While bugs in their bow ties convene for a cheer.
'Maybe we'll grow into something quite tall!'
And the bushes all giggle, 'Well, we won't at all!'

A party of fungi sneaks onto the scene,
Mushroom hats boast loud, they're regal and keen.
They toast to the leaves and their fluttering mirth,
Cheering for friendships that bubble from earth.

With laughter and joy in their intertwined ways,
A tapestry woven, each stitch sings of plays.
Let's leap and let's dance, for there's magic around,
In embraces from soil, pure fun can be found!

The Aria of the Underground

Beneath the dirt, a concert ignites,
Worms with a flair perform wiggly flights.
The roots throw confetti, a glorious sight,
As beetles recite with delight on a flight!

A ladybug conductor waves tiny arms,
While moles drumming beats are a cause for alarms.
The ants in their platoon march stiff and right,
Prancing around like they're ready to fight!

The fun-loving critters all gather and play,
For a famished fox what a feast they display.
'Join us for tea!' croaked a frog in a suit,
While gophers serve cupcakes, so sweet and so cute!

The aria echoes, a melody grand,
A spectacular show with no need for a band.
So come to the burrows where laughter won't cease,
With raucous joy, they compose their own peace!

The Network Below

In a garden where gossip flows,
The carrots and beans strike silly poses.
Radishes giggle with their red tops high,
While peas forecast rain from the clear blue sky.

Worms in their tunnels, a band on parade,
Belting out tunes while they're never afraid.
They wiggle and dance, what a sight to see,
In the network below, there's wild jubilee!

Under the soil, they throw a grand ball,
As plants sip their drinks from the rainwater wall.
With laughter and fun, they grow day by day,
In this wacky garden, they're here to play!

So next time you dig, give a cheer to the crew,
For the network below has its own kind of view.
In the world underground, it's all such a score,
Every root, every stem, is a friend we adore!

The Recital of the Hidden

In the shade where no sunlight can reach,
The mushrooms have gathered for quite the speech.
They wiggle and giggle on top of their caps,
While the clovers all tap dance in fancy mishaps.

The kudzu climbs up, a diva so grand,
With vines that stretch out, she has plenty of band.
The snails hold a contest, who's slowest of all,
As the critters cheer loudly, loving the brawl.

'Neath the surface, a party unfolds,
With secrets and stories that never grow old.
Each critter a jester, they spin quite the tale,
Under the surface, friendships set sail!

So when springtime is here and the garden comes bright,
Think of the hidden that dance through the night.
For in every small plot, there's a rich, funny lore,
That whispers of laughter in a world we adore.

The Unfurled Connections

In the tangled mess where the weeds try to play,
The dandelions debate who'll save the day.
With their golden crowns and their fluffy white hair,
They plot up their mischief with nary a care.

Vines climb high just to see what's ahead,
While twining round fences, they laugh with the thread.
The petals all shout, 'It's a party, my friend!
Join in on the fun, let the games never end!'

In this jumbled fiesta where all misfits thrive,
A squash says, 'Why not? Let's all just dive!'
As veggies unite, forming the greatest show,
In the unfurled connections, the laughter will grow!

So if you're feeling down, take a peek underneath,
There's a world full of giggles that will give you great peace.
Amongst all the chaos, a joyous rapport,
In the garden's embrace, we can't help but roar!

The Roots of our Echoes

Down in the deep where the soil is thick,
The tomatoes are squeaking, oh, what a trick!
They joke about salsa with zest from the vine,
While garlic gives pointers, 'Don't be shy, just shine!'

The radicchio rolls, it's a hit and a miss,
With peppers in tow, sharing laughter and bliss.
As they reminisce 'bout the weather last fall,
Their banter is grand, and they're having a ball!

From the whispers of sprouts to the growls of the weeds,
They echo their stories like rippling creeds.
In the depths of this world where the laughter is free,
The roots of our echoes are alive with glee!

So, lend an ear to the murmurs below,
For beneath our feet, there's a vibrant glow.
In the garden where silliness always ignites,
The echoes of joy dance on magical nights!

Thunder in the Soil

Deep beneath, the whispers play,
Worms and critters dance all day.
With every shudder, up they come,
Making earth their thunder drum.

The daisies giggle, grass does sway,
As roots snicker in their way.
A beetle shouts, 'Let's have a race!'
While mushrooms laugh, all over the place.

Beneath the surface, chaos reigns,
With gophers sharing silly gains.
Though no one sees the fun unfold,
The soil's secret is pure gold.

So if you hear a rumble and roar,
It's just the earth, ready for more!
With every shake, giggles in store,
Mother Nature's wild folklore.

Shadows of the Ancients

In the dark, the old trees mumble,
As squirrels dance and tumble.
Their shadows stretch to share a joke,
While owls hoot, they laugh and poke.

The wise old roots, they shake and grin,
'We've seen it all, come join our kin!'
Past lovers' whispers, fights galore,
What ancient tales can trees explore?

With branches wide, they play charades,
'The wind's too strong—let's make some shades!'
The ants march in, with tiny feet,
'Bring on the story, we can't be beat!'

So every shadow holds a tale,
Of secret brands and ancient wail.
Just listen close, you might hear more,
Of laughing roots that never bore.

Unyielding Embrace of the Forgotten

Beneath the stones, the laughter flows,
With mossy hugs and soil-y throws.
The rocks recall their ancient chat,
'Remember when we were all that?'

A turtle crawls, with tales to tell,
Of shady days and rainy spells.
While snails, they ponder on their fate,
'Let's race tomorrow, but don't be late!'

The ferns stand proud, heads held high,
Claiming 'We bloom, though none pass by!'
With every wind, secrets are shared,
In this embrace, none are spared.

So tiptoe through the forgotten lane,
You might sing songs of joy and pain.
For roots and rocks, friends evermore,
In the garden, laughter will soar.

The Voiced Legacy of the Timber

The tall trees yell, 'We've so much to say!'
With branches that twist and sway.
'With every ring, we tell a tale,'
Of pines and oaks that will prevail.

The woodpecker knocks, 'Hey, join my band!'
As squirrels audition across the land.
The trunks chime in, a chorus loud,
'We're the best timber, strong and proud!'

Old saplings giggle, trying to dream,
'Let's start a forest talent scheme!'
And all around, the creatures cheer,
For nature's music is always near.

So next time you're under a leafy crew,
Just listen close, it's singing for you.
In every whisper, laughter rings,
From timber's heart, joy always springs.

Vibrations of the Ancients

In the ground where secrets lie,
Twirling worms and spiders sigh.
Moles with hats, they dance and jig,
Claiming turf, they feel so big.

Listen close, a crackling sound,
It's the chatter of the ground.
Old tree stumps chuckle, share a joke,
As the wind gives them a poke.

Beneath the soil, a party stirs,
Dancing roots and giggling furs.
A worm plays tunes, a beetle sings,
While ants march by with funny things.

So next time you plant or dig away,
Remember they're laughing in their play.
For nature knows how to caper loud,
With each little creature feeling proud.

Rhythms of the Hidden

Beneath the grass, where shadows creep,
A busy colony, no time for sleep.
They tap their feet, a funky beat,
The ants have formed a dance-off fleet.

Moles in tuxedos steal the show,
They twirl and twist, put on a glow.
Raccoons juggling acorns high,
While squirrels mock them, oh me, oh my!

The trees sway gently, joining in,
Tickling bugs make the fun begin.
A caterpillar DJs, spinning tunes,
As crickets chirp their happy boons.

And when the sun starts sinking low,
The forest pulses with its flow.
Watch it giggle, see it whirl,
In this hidden world, watch them twirl!

The Pulse of the Earth

Feel the thumping of the ground,
Where silly critters roam around.
Frogs in bow ties croak with flair,
While leaping lizards hide in their lair.

Gophers gather for a spree,
Digging trenches, being free!
Lizards chat about their style,
Doing the worm, all the while.

Roots are tangled, full of cheer,
Swaying softly, nothing to fear.
The night is young, the fun's begun,
As fireflies flash and insects run.

They dance beneath the moonlit skies,
With nature's laughter as the prize.
In this pulse, alive and bold,
The earth brings joys untold.

Beneath the Bark

Underneath the sturdy brown,
There's a party going down.
Woodpeckers tapping, beat of the drum,
While squirrels tease—"Here they come!"

Caterpillars wear their hats,
Throwing shade at passing rats.
Mice with glasses read the scrolls,
They gossip about tree trunk trolls.

Fungi sprout in sparkly blues,
Spreading cheer and funny views.
While shrooms grip 'round a tiny stage,
They perform like the best of sage.

So if you peek beneath the bark,
You'll find a world that leaves its mark.
With laughter echoing through the night,
In this woodland, all feels right.

Currents Through Clay

In the garden, plants do sway,
Worms practicing hip-hop all day.
Clay gets muddy, a squishy dance,
Potted pals take a wild chance.

Flowers gossip beneath the sun,
Bees mistaken a flower for fun.
Bumblebees buzzing with flair so grand,
Polka-dot petals in a jamming band.

Rain drops join in, tapping a beat,
Nature's rhythm, oh so sweet.
Each puddle a stage for a splashing show,
While frogs leap high, stealing the flow.

And when the sun dips, quiet prevails,
The moon whispers, spinning silly tales.
In gardens, it's never a boring sight,
Just clay, bugs, and plants getting it right.

Sinews of the Silent

In the stillness, whispers play,
The silent trees have much to say.
Boughs stretch out, in "Hello!" cheer,
While roots gossip, pricking the ear.

A squirrel prances, a nut in tow,
He stops to listen, then puts on a show.
Branches chuckle as leaves shimmy down,
Spinning round, making quite the crown.

Mice waltz under a mushroom's shade,
Fungi giggle, an underground parade.
Nature's secrets in a comic twist,
With each little dance, something's missed.

Through the silence, humor flows,
Nature's joy in quiet shows.
With sinews strong, yet so absurd,
Laughter thrives without a word.

The Language of the Timbers

Wooden giants shuffle in grace,
In their whispers, there's a funny space.
Bark calls out like it knows the score,
As acorns tumble, oh what a chore!

Saplings lean in for gossip and fun,
Sharing tales of the hot summer sun.
While branches stretch in warming embrace,
Creating a stage, a natural base.

The logs laugh as they tell their tale,
Of storms and critters, an amusing trail.
Moss joins in, a fuzzy cheer,
Encouraging saplings to persevere.

In the forest, the language flows,
Between the timbers, laughter grows.
They dance in shadows, under a tree,
Where nature's humor is wild and free.

The Unbreakable Bond

Two blades of grass form a friendship true,
Laughing off raindrops that stick like glue.
They twist and twirl in the light breeze,
Swaying together with perfect ease.

Dandelions giggle in their sunny hue,
While thistles stab jokes about morning dew.
Together they flourish, side by side,
In this garden where laughs never hide.

The sun plays tricks, a shadow tease,
Laughter erupts as they sway with ease.
A snail zooms past on a wild, wild ride,
Pausing a moment, laughter as his guide.

In this bond, a joyful cheer,
Every tickle from bugs brings them near.
An unbreakable link, with giggles and grins,
In the dance of growth, the fun never ends.

www.ingramcontent.com/pod-product-compliance
Lightning Source LLC
Chambersburg PA
CBHW051632160426
43209CB00004B/617